THE OFFICIAL BOOK

THE OFFICIAL BOOK

KATE THORNTON AND JANE PRESTON

Virgin

First published in 1998 by Virgin Books,
an imprint of Virgin Publishing Ltd
332 Ladbroke Grove, London W10 5AH

A catalogue record for this book is available from the British Library

ISBN: 0 7535 0297 6

Printed and bound by Butler & Tanner

Designed by Slatter-Anderson

CONTENTS

WANTED

FIVE BAD BOYS WITH THE POWER TO ROCK YA!

A year ago, at the height of the Girl Power movement, two men decided that British pop music needed kicking into shape.

They knew they had the know-how and the ability to put together one of the world's most exciting bands since the launch of the Spice Girls – after all, they were the men who'd put Scary, Baby, Sporty, Posh and Ginger together in the first place.

With this in mind, they decided that an edgy, attitude-led band that 'walked it as it talked it' could blow the brains of pop lovers. And so they created Five.

These men are Bob and Chris Herbert, a father and son partnership who run Safe Management and they're the 'Daddies' of the band, if you like. While they work together as a team they have separate roles, with Bob taking care of the band's business affairs and Chris looking after the creative side of management.

They conceived Five, gave birth to them and have since nurtured the band through the teething pains of their infancy in the pop world.

And, like any proud parents, they are convinced their offspring will go on to rule the world.

"When we came up with the idea to form a 'lad band' we knew that there was a gap in the market. There were loads of boy bands in the charts who were doing okay, but there wasn't an all-male group that was exciting in the way that Take That once were," says Chris, 26, who works with his father from the Safe HQ in Surrey.

"We didn't want a band that pretended to live an unbelievably squeaky-clean existence and who would sing songs as bland as their image. We wanted to put together a group that was real. We'd already created the biggest act Britain had ever seen with the Spice Girls and we knew that we could do it again."

Feeling confident they launched a nation-wide search via a string of auditions held up and down the country – amid a frenzy of media attention. "We decided to put an ad in *The Stage* newspaper, as we had done when we were auditioning for the Spice Girls," explains Bob, 55, who also worked with 80s pop sensation Bros.

"Up until then, no-one knew that we'd put the Spice Girls together and suddenly it hit the press – the media went crazy for the auditions. The headlines read 'Spice Boys Wanted', 'Boy Power!' and we were being talked about on every TV and radio station. Thousands of lads turned up – it was madness."

Unbeknown to the crowds who stormed the auditions, Bob and Chris had already secured record company interest for the lucky applicants with RCA Records – the label that gave us Take That.

Chris had begun work on the foundations of the group with RCA's A&R (Artists and Repertoire) man Simon Cowell months earlier and, with Simon in place, Bob and Chris set about seeking out the stars of tomorrow.

"We knew what we were looking for," remembers Bob, "but there was no guarantee that we were going to find it. It was more a case of the right guys finding us. And we got lucky. Very lucky."

SCOTT'S STORY : "My uncle told me about the auditions, but I almost didn't go. I was at Sylvia Young's Agency at the time, having just left school, and I remember lying in bed with a hangover on the morning of the audition saying to my dad 'I'm not going, it's bound to be rubbish.' But I changed my mind. Don't ask me why – something just told me that I could miss out if I didn't go.

"I met J in the queue and we hit it off straight away. We did the dance audition together and we both had to sing a song we'd already prepared – I did Glenn Medeiros's 'Nothing's Gonna Change My Love For You', which is a wicked song. But I don't think J was convinced!"

J'S STORY: "My first thought, when I heard about the audition from my girlfriend, was that it would be a laugh and might help me get a foot in the door of the music industry. I'd been writing and recording as a solo artist for two years and was having no luck getting a deal, so I decided to go along and do my best.

"When I got there, TV crews and journalists were everywhere. I met Scott in the queue and couldn't believe it when he got through the dance audition because he barely moved!

"I would tell you what I sang, but I've vowed that it's a secret which me, the lads, Chris and Bob will have to take to the grave with us!"

RICHARD'S STORY: "I'd seen the ad in the papers too and my mum said, 'You've got to go for it'. I was a little unsure about how I'd get on so I didn't tell anyone I was going. So you can imagine my surprise when that Sunday, after I'd come back from the pub with my mates, my mum told me there was a picture of me in the newspapers with some of the lads from the audition.

"Bob and Chris sent me a letter, a week later, asking me to come for the recall. I sang George Michael's 'Freedom' and was so nervous I was shaking. That was the first time I met the rest of the guys – and within hours of meeting we were told we'd got the job. I couldn't believe it."

SEAN'S STORY: "I got there, sang one of my own songs called 'Dream Land' and that was it – I went home again. I heard I'd got the recall when I came home from school after football. Mum told me Chris had left a message. I thought,'Yeah – sorted. My time has come'.

"I think Chris was worried that I wouldn't turn up to the second audition, because I'm really laid-back and must have sounded not bothered

"AS SOON AS THE FIVE OF US PERFORMED TOGETHER IT WAS SO OBVIOUS THAT WE WERE WELL-SUITED."

on the phone. But I was. It was a rare moment of excitement – I think I might have even smiled!"

ABS' STORY: "My singing teacher at the Italia Conti Stage School told me about the audition and as soon as

the five of us performed together it was so obvious that we were well-suited.

"Chris told me at my first audition that they were only looking for four people, but they soon changed their minds and gave us the job. By the time we left the second audition we looked like we'd been together for

six months instead of six minutes and, to top it all off, Simon Cowell offered us a deal on the spot. It was amazing!"

From the start, Bob and Chris only planned to have four members in the band because they were eager to steer clear of the conventional five-piece pop phenomenon. But they liked all five lads and, by the end of the second audition, were at a loss as to who they should lose from the line-up.

"It was impossible trying to decide who to let go. When we saw them perform as a five-piece and they sounded and looked so right we knew there was no way we could afford to lose any of them," says Bob. "They were a

group before we even told them they were a group, it was obvious they would work well together.

"And that's how Five were born. The rest, as they say, will be history."

FIVE LADS

+ ONE HOUSE = MEN BEHAVING BADLY!

For as long as he can remember, J has dreamed of the day when he would hear the magic words "We'd like to sign you up for a record deal and move you into a house in London – all expenses paid, you understand".

"I thought I'd died and gone to heaven," explains the bearded one, of the moment Bob and Chris told the band they'd organized a three-bedroomed house in Surrey for the lads to move into.

It was an arrangement that had worked well for Safe Management, when they'd signed the Spice Girls two years previously, and was one they felt would prove equally successful for Sean, Abs, J, Scott and Rich.

With the ink still wet on the Five recording contract, they told the boys they could move in on 10 May 1997. It was a day that none of them would forget.

"Our first problem was a simple case of geography. Sean was from Leeds, Richard from Birmingham, J from Warrington, Scott from Essex and only Abs was based in central London," says Chris.

"You also have to remember that they didn't know each other. We were expecting five complete strangers to suddenly click as a unit, so the best way for them to get to know each other was for them to live together. It was a chance for them to iron out the creases in their personalities before the hard work started.

"It was also a bonding experience – a dress rehearsal for what lay ahead. There was work to be done and nothing was going to be achieved until the lads felt they knew and trusted each other. We were killing two birds

"WE TURNED A PERFECTLY NICE HOUSE INTO A PIGSTY." 5 JASON

with one stone. Besides, we needed to have all five of them together to save on cab bills if nothing else!"

Sean was the first to arrive at the house on a family housing estate in Camberley, Surrey – and true to character he saw this as the perfect opportunity for bagging his own room.

"You don't have to be Einstein to realise that five lads sharing a three-bedroomed house means that only one lad gets his own room," remembers Sean. "First come, first served, Bob and Chris said, so I moved my stuff into the box room quicker than you can say 'Sean, would you like your own room?'."

J and Rich arrived together and were quick to claim the biggest room in the house as their own. They had both said tearful goodbyes to their friends and families and were experiencing mixed emotions when they pulled up at their new address.

"Moving into the house was memorable for me - and quite sad," recalls J, who at the time was living with his 27-year-old girlfriend of two years. "I remember leaving my girlfriend and her crying, saying things between us

"I FELT OPTIMISTIC ABOUT MOVING. I KNEW IT WAS GOING TO BE AN EXPERIENCE I WOULD REMEMBER FOR THE REST OF MY LIFE."

5 ABS

would change and that our relationship would never last.

"It was real case of mixed emotions because I was sad to be leaving her, but part of me was really excited – and I felt guilty about that. I was pretty messed up by the time I got to the house."

"I was a mess too," remembers Rich. "When we arrived at the house I was really nervous, which isn't like me. I'm normally the most confident person in the world, but I came over all shy with the rest of the band and worried they wouldn't like me."

Abs took the move in his stride. "I wanted to get to know the lads and I was looking forward to living with them, but it wasn't such a wrench for me because my mum's was less than an hour away if I wanted to go home," he says. "I felt optimistic. I knew it was going to be the best thing that ever happened to me."

For Scott though, there were tears shed on the doorstep – only they weren't his own. "My mum came to the house and, as we said goodbye, she wouldn't stop crying," laughs the motor-mouth. "From the moment we auditioned for Five we've had a film crew following us, making a documentary, and they were there getting it all on camera. If they hadn't been there I would have cried too.

"Like J and Abs I was also in a relationship, so it was hard leaving my girlfriend – not to mention all the comforts of home. But secretly I was loving every minute of it...until the arguments started, that is."

It was to be expected. Nothing short of a miracle would have prevented the rows, the tension and the verbal abuse that was to follow. The lads were rehearsing by day and when they returned to the house by night – feeling exhausted – they had to learn how to live with each other.

Walls were punched, tempers were frayed, beers were consumed, and in between the bickering and niggling they had the time of their lives.

"At first we had to sort out our differences," says Scott. "Sean was lazy, I was too mouthy, J was moody, the way Rich kept pushing his hair off his face drove us crazy."

"What got me more than anything was the mess," says J, who is the most house-proud of the group. "I used to get up at 5 a.m. to do the housework if people were coming round for meetings because I was so ashamed of the state of the place.

"I think Sean washed up three times during the whole time we lived there and it took Scott three months to work out how to use the washing machine. The bins were always overflowing, there were clothes everywhere, plates of takeaway all over the place – in short, we turned

"AT FIRST WE HAD TO SORT OUT OUR DIFFERENCES. SEAN WAS LAZY, I WAS TOO MOUTHY, J WAS MOODY, THE WAY RICH KEPT PUSHING HIS HAIR OFF HIS FACE DROVE US CRAZY." 5 SCOTT

a perfectly nice house into a pigsty."

"When I moved in I didn't have a clue how to use anything except the kettle," confirms Scott, who has since been educated in the art of housework by J.

"I was the only one who ever cooked and I only cooked twice," says Rich, who ventured as far as a curry and a bowl of pasta. "I think Scott might have attempted a pizza once – he's a junk food junkie – but I'm not sure if he got it from the petrol station or cooked it himself.

"I USED TO GET UP AT 5 A.M. TO DO THE HOUSEWORK IF PEOPLE WERE COMING ROUND FOR MEETINGS BECAUSE I WAS SO ASHAMED OF THE STATE OF THE PLACE."

JASON

To be honest, we've only ever been shopping for food three times. Most of the time Bob and Chris send us supplies, it's easier that way – otherwise we end up arguing about who wants what."

But the lads didn't just row with each other. The neighbours got a piece of the action too – to such a degree that Five would later be featured in an ITV documentary series, aptly entitled *Neighbours From Hell.*

"Bob and Marilyn, our neighbours on one side really liked us," recalls Scott. "They were lovely. We borrowed sugar and a rolling pin from them and I'd like to say sorry we forgot to bring it back. But the neighbours the other side hated us."

"I can see their point though," counters J. "They were a family with a new-born baby, so I can understand why they objected to the constant noise, not only from us but also from the fans who started hanging around the house.

"They reacted exactly how we would have reacted if we'd moved next door to ourselves. We can't blame them. In fact, I'd like to say sorry to them. We meant to get them some flowers as an apology when we left, but never got round to it."

Not surprisingly, when the lads' six month lease on the house came up, they were asked to leave. By then the landlords had received complaints from the police, the Environmental Health office, the council and many tenants in the street.

It was decided that a detached property would be more suited to their up-all-night life style and – unlike their arrival – no tears were shed when they packed up and moved to their new abode.

FIVE ALIVE!

THE TOUR, THE AWARDS AND THE TOP TEN

Had it not been for winning the *Smash Hits* Best New Tour Act Award, the pop world may have been denied two of the biggest acts to have stormed the charts this decade.

Both Boyzone and the Backstreet Boys were launched on the back of this prestigious award, which is voted for by the thousands of fans who pack out arenas across England, Ireland, Scotland and Wales in November when the *Smash Hits* annual tour comes to town.

It seemed only fitting then, that – just one month before the release of Five's debut single 'Slam Dunk (Da Funk)', which was fast gathering radio airplay and press attention – the band should be amongst the 1997 contenders, the winner of which would be revealed at the televised *Smash Hits* Poll Winners Party.

For Five, the *Smash Hits* tour was a crucial test, presenting them with their first opportunity to find out if, as a band, they could really cut it on stage.

"Our only performance up until then had been on the Radio One Roadshow," says Rich. "Although it had gone brilliantly, it was something else to be playing to thousands of fans with some of the biggest acts in the business.

"We knew we were up against two really good bands, Chill and 98°, and we were quite nervous about how we'd be received. But it went better than any of us could ever have imagined. We couldn't believe the response. It was fantastic."

Off stage, Five were also netting the majority of attention. While the lads travelled to each venue on the

FIVE SIGNING TO RCA IN JUNE 1997

branded double-decker *Smash Hits* tour bus with the likes of Peter Andre, Jimmy Ray, 911, N-Tyce, Kavana and Aqua – it was the name Five that the fans were chanting every time they arrived at an arena or hotel.

The entire *Smash Hits* entourage – which totalled more than one hundred people – also provided the lads with the perfect excuse to get down to their favourite pastime – serious after-hours partying. "It was a real laugh sitting up all night drinking with everyone on the tour and getting to know so many new people," says Scott, who celebrated his 18th birthday on the road. "We weren't fazed by being with some of the biggest names in pop because everybody was really chilled."

"Yeah," adds Rich. "It brought us all closer together. He'll kill me for mentioning this, but Scott got really drunk on his 18th birthday – and we still don't know exactly where he spent the night!"

While the lads were enjoying themselves on- and off-stage, the votes were piling up in anticipation of the big day when all would be revealed at the *Smash Hits* Poll Winners Party at the London Arena.

If anybody had told Sean, J, Rich, Scott and Abs, just six months earlier that they would end up playing on the same stage as Janet Jackson, the Spice Girls, Texas, Celine Dion and All Saints, they would probably have laughed.

Indeed, they would have laughed even harder if they'd been told that, at the *Smash Hits* Poll Winners Party on 30 November at London Docklands Arena in front of 12,000 screaming fans, they would hear the words 'And the

"ALL CHRIS HAD TOLD ME WAS THAT WE WEREN'T IN THE TOP 15 – AND AS THEY COUNTED DOWN FROM 20 TO 15 I WAS NEARLY IN TEARS." (5) SCOTT

winner of the Best New Tour Act 1997 is...FIVE!'

"I used to watch the Poll Winners Party every year and wish it were me up there," says Abs. "I couldn't believe it when it actually happened."

As the lads arrived at the after-show party at London's Trocadero they were stunned to find hoards of fans there calling for their autographs and a bank of photographers shouting for pictures.

"It was brilliant," says Rich, "just like when you see film stars arriving at the Oscars, there were camera flashes popping everywhere. The photographers were shouting 'Over here lads, over here'. We were made up."

For the band it was the ultimate proof that they had what it takes. For Bob and Chris it was vindication that, when it comes to it, they have the best eye in the business for putting together great talent. They were almost there...all that remained to be seen, one week later, was how well 'Slam Dunk (Da Funk)' would do in the charts.

In the week following the *Smash Hits* awards the lads worked like they never had before, appearing on some of the biggest radio and television shows in the country to promote 'Slam'.

"We did *Live & Kicking* and chinned Mr Blobby!" recounts Scott. "Then there was *This Morning* with Richard and Judy and Richard was really nice to us. We also did *The Big Breakfast* and that was a laugh, but the one show we wanted to do was *Top Of The Pops* – and to get on that you have to get in the charts."

But the buzz on 'Slam' was good and Radio One DJ, Dave Pearce, came on board as a big supporter – as did most of the press. "We'd like to say a massive thanks to Dave," says Abs. "He was cool and did everything he could to help us. The press support was brilliant too – we were in the *Sunday Times, Smash Hits*, the *Daily Mirror*, the *News Of The World, More!, TV Hits* and *Bliss* to name a few.

While there was every indication that 'Slam' could possibly chart in the Top 20, the lads never anticipated it would go straight in at...Number 10.

When the record company phoned with the news, the band reacted true to character. Ever cool and collected, Abs was so confident of the single's success that he barely lifted his eyes from his Playstation, Rich brushed away the tears as he celebrated in his room with his brother and Sean slept through it all, as only Sean could.

Scott was the only member of the band who was out of the house when the good news came through, which proved a 'too-good-to-miss' opportunity for J to do a massive wind-up. "There was me, Scott and Chris in the van listening to the charts as we were driving down to do the *Clothes Show Live* exhibition in Birmingham where we

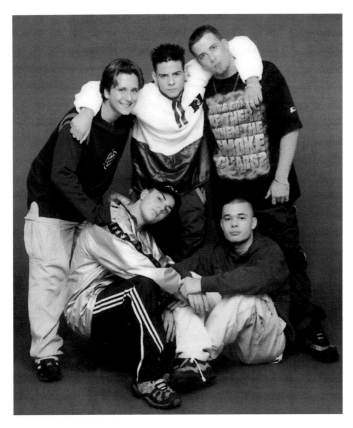

"IT WAS BRILLIANT. JUST LIKE WHEN YOU SEE FILM STARS ARRIVING AT THE OSCARS, THERE WERE CAMERA FLASHES POPPING EVERYWHERE."

were due to meet the others," explains J.

"Only Scott didn't know that we already knew we were Number 10. To make the wind-up authentic I kept saying, 'Please, God, let us be Number 17', then next record, 'Please, God, I'll do anything if you make us Number 16'. I could barely keep myself from cracking up."

"All Chris had told me was that we weren't in the Top 15 - and as they counted down from 20 to 15 I was nearly in tears," recalls Scott. "Then it got to 15 and it wasn't us. I was distraught, ready to burst into tears. I had my head between my knees and I was telling Chris I wanted to punch him and that the band was rubbish...then I heard, 'and at Number 10 an impressive debut for Five...'."

"Scott was screaming his head off," laughs J, "and we were screaming, 'We already knew! We already knew. Oh, my God!!' It was so funny."

The icing on the cake came in the form of an invitation the following day to appear on that week's edition of *Top Of The Pops*. It was something all five lads had dreamt of.

"It was mad going into the studio," remembers Sean, "it's so much smaller than it appears on TV. We were so chuffed to be there, I had to keep pinching myself."

SEAN CONLON

Talented, funny and definitely up for it...

SEAN CONLON may be the baby of the group, but you'd never know it. With a sense of humour that's as dry as a bone and a flair for song-writing that has impressed even Phil Collins, his youth can only be an advantage.

Born in Horsworth, Leeds in 1981, he grew up on a tough council estate with his mum, Kate, two sisters, Charlotte and Katrina, brother Dominic and half-brother John. His parents split when he was nine and his dad Dennis now lives in Southport.

Like Abs, Sean is perceived to be quiet and reserved, but get to know him and you soon realize he's brimming with a laid-back confidence that only the seriously talented can afford – so listen up...

"The rest of the band tell me I'm lazy, shy and quiet, but I think I'm just very laid-back. It's just that nothing really gets me going, except for music – which has always been the love of my life.

"My dad is a drummer, my sister plays guitar and my brother is a DJ so there was always music playing in our house. In fact, my earliest memory is of me performing songs I'd made up in our back garden with a toy guitar I'd been given for my fourth birthday.

"But it wasn't until I was nine that music really kicked into my life. I'd been given a keyboard for Christmas and started writing songs (my first was about how really I

ALREADY PERFORMING AT 2 YEARS OLD!

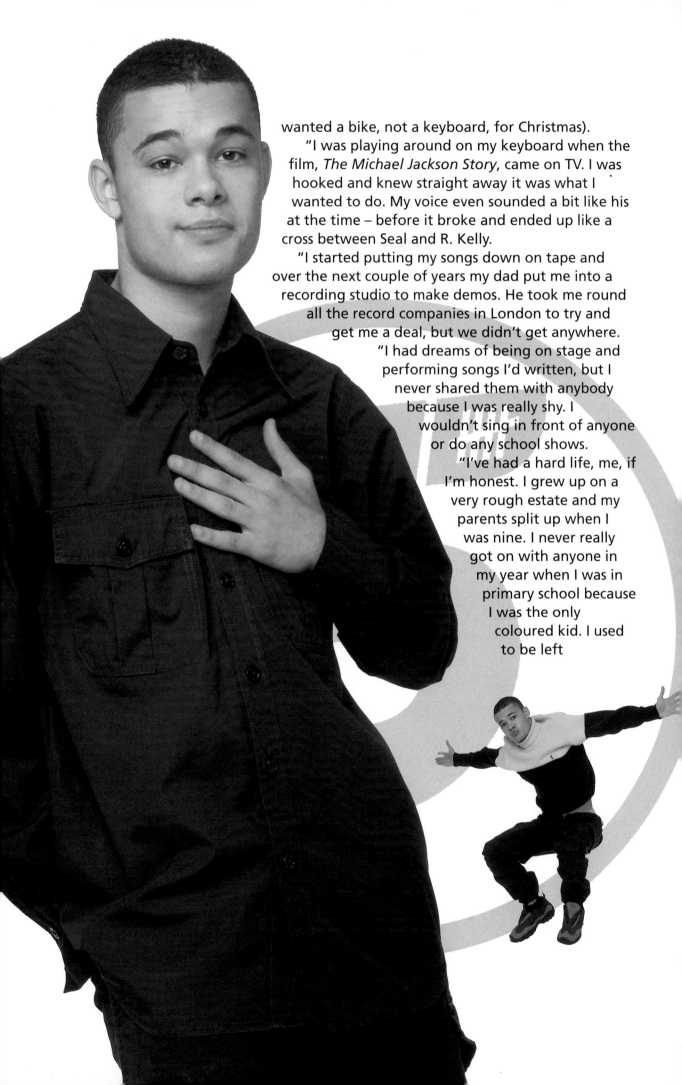

wanted a bike, not a keyboard, for Christmas).

"I was playing around on my keyboard when the film, *The Michael Jackson Story*, came on TV. I was hooked and knew straight away it was what I wanted to do. My voice even sounded a bit like his at the time – before it broke and ended up like a cross between Seal and R. Kelly.

"I started putting my songs down on tape and over the next couple of years my dad put me into a recording studio to make demos. He took me round all the record companies in London to try and get me a deal, but we didn't get anywhere.

"I had dreams of being on stage and performing songs I'd written, but I never shared them with anybody because I was really shy. I wouldn't sing in front of anyone or do any school shows.

"I've had a hard life, me, if I'm honest. I grew up on a very rough estate and my parents split up when I was nine. I never really got on with anyone in my year when I was in primary school because I was the only coloured kid. I used to be left out of things all the time and get called brownie or nigger. In the end I became mates with kids in the year above because they used to stick up for me.

"I never worked at school because I was only ever interested in music. My school reports always said 'Sean is capable of doing well but he gives up too easily and is distracted by his friends. He's always late.' I was quite bad really.

"I went to a Catholic school and the rest of the kids were all a bit posher than me. Because I had a skinhead they were scared of me – I had a reputation for being hard and was considered to be one of the rough ones.

"It was during my first year at secondary school that I developed my first crush, on a girl called Helena. This other lad liked her too and brought her chocolates and stuff. But it was more like 'I like you, do you like me or not? If you don't then I'll see you later'. I used to write songs about girls I fancied – but I never told them.

"I've only really had one proper girlfriend and it could have been great, but I messed up. I went on holiday and met this other girl. I came home and started acting differently towards her because I felt guilty and eventually it fizzled out.

"Music was the only thing that stopped me going off the rails. My school suggested I enter the Young Composer of the Year competition when I was 14, so my dad sent my tape off and one of my songs, 'Everything In The World', got into the top three of the competition. I had to come down to London for the final that was hosted at Earl's Court in front of a panel of judges, including Phil Collins.

"When they called my name out as the winner of the 13 to 16 age group it was like 'Yes!'. Winning felt really good. It was the biggest day of my life...until I joined Five that is.

"Before I could join the group I had to leave school, which wasn't as easy as it sounds because I was only 15. Bob had to clear it with the local authorities for me to leave early and study with a private tutor. Then, when it came to exam time, Bob flew me back home to sit my exams.

"I thought Christmas had come early – I got to leave school to go and live in a nice house with a bunch of lads I'd just got a record deal with; I wasn't complaining!"

"I HAD DREAMS OF BEING ON STAGE AND PERFORMING SONGS I'D WRITTEN, BUT I NEVER SHARED THEM WITH ANYBODY."

FACTFILE

SEAN

1. **Sex** Of course.

2. **Drinking** Love it.

3. **Politics** Load of rubbish and uninteresting.

4. **Music** Is my life.

5. **Fashion** Not interested – I dress in what I like.

6. **Money** Want loads of it.

7. **Fame** False, and just an illusion to make money.

8. **Sport** Used to love football, running and mostly rugby league. Then I gave them all up.

9. **Women** Can't do with them, can't do without them.

10. **Love** Makes everything go right. It makes you happier and stronger. It is also hard to let go of it.

11. **Biggest extravagance** Having fun, drinking, and whatever.

12. **Best buy** First keyboard.

13. **Favourite accessory** My keyboard.

14. **Favourite hang-out** Anywhere with soul music playing and with people I'm close to.

15. **Favourite romantic moment** Being somewhere quiet, miles away from noise and people. Getting to know somebody really well, and becoming close.

16. **Worst buy** Cigarettes.

17. **Love girls who** Care a lot and are faithful, and stand by you whatever.

18. **Favourite take-away** Chinese, Indian, everything really.

19. **Favourite record of all time** There are too many songs that I love.

20. **Worst record of all time** Something cheesy like Mr Blobby or Teletubbies.

21. **Worst habit** Having a messy room, and just leaving it.

Favourite romantic moment: Being somewhere quiet miles away from noise and people, getting to know somebody really well, and getting close.

Worst buy: Cigarettes

Love girls who: care alot and are faithful, and stand by you whatever.

Hate girls who:

Favourite take-away: chinese, indian, aswell as everything really.

Favourite record of all time: There's too many songs that I love

Worst Record of all time: Something cheesy like blobby or telly-tubbies.

Worst habit: having a messy room, and just leaving it.

Favourite part of the female body: Mouth and eyes.

Monthly mobile phone bill: I don't have one. I don't want one 'til I'm a little older. It makes you too available and sometimes people automatically think you're showing off.

Worst job ever had: paper round its slave labour.

One thing I'd change about myself: Nothing. I don't love myself, but I am proud and happy with the way I am.

㉒ **Favourite part of the female body** Mouth and eyes.

㉓ **Monthly mobile phone bill** I don't have one. I don't want one 'til I'm a little older. It makes you too available and sometimes people automatically think you're showing off.

㉔ **Worst job ever had** Paper round - it's slave labour.

㉕ **One thing I'd change about myself** Nothing. I don't love myself, but I am proud and happy with the way I am.

㉖ **Biggest regret** I don't really have any.

㉗ **Proudest achievement** Winning Young Composer of the Year 1995 and Best New Tour Act of 1997 (*Smash Hits*).

JASON
BROWN

Mean and moody or just misunderstood? You decide.

BANGING MY FIRST DRUM, 2 YEARS OLD.

ME AT SIX YEARS OLD, DRESSED FOR FOOTBALL TRAINING.

As the eldest member of Five, **JASON BROWN** has assumed the position of band leader from day one – a role to which he is well-suited. He was born on 13 June 1976 in Aldershot, but went on to live all over the country, and even Canada and Germany briefly, with his parents, Marilyn and Justin, and elder sister, Donna.

Because of his no-nonsense, speak-your-mind attitude, those who meet J always have lots to say about him – but here's what he says about himself...

"I'm a music-loving, sociable person who's prone to mood swings. At least, I'd say that was a pretty accurate description of myself. As a kid I was always banging a set of saucepans and singing to myself. In fact I can't remember a time when music hasn't been the biggest passion in my life.

"The first record I bought was by Doug E. Fresh And The Get Fresh Crew, it was really early hip-hop and it influenced me so much. I've always been into hip-hop and 80s soul music and I went through phases of being into chart music, but not on the same scale as someone like Scott – he is 'Mr Cheesy Pop'.

"I used to do robotics with my mates at school on 'show and tell' days. There were all these kids with flower presses and rabbits and me and my mates in our

Kappa tracksuits doing robotics on bits of cardboard!

"Because of my dad's work in the Forces we moved house 13 times, but it was never a problem for me – I enjoyed changing school. I was born in Aldershot, then we moved around the Merseyside and Lancashire area, then to Germany for a few years, then Canada, Warrington, Farnborough and back to Warrington where we stayed until I moved to Surrey with the band.

"Living in so many places has made me more outgoing and able to make friends quickly. I've always been the class joker, eager to entertain. At school I mucked about because I hated being there so much. Waking up in the morning, knowing I had to go, used to make me feel physically sick. I think it comes from having a problem with people telling me what to do.

"Schoolwork never interested me, especially when I went to sixth form college to re-sit a couple of GCSEs. I only did re-sits because it gave me enough free time to work on my demo tapes. However, I did end up with five Grade B O-Levels and four GCSEs.

"I was in my element when I got my first recording studio while I was living with my ex-girlfriend. She was so good to me and paid for the studio equipment.

"I spent hours making demos which I sent to all the major record companies, but they all turned me down because my material wasn't commercial enough – it was so depressing. People kept telling me I should join a band, but I wouldn't entertain the idea because I was so determined to make it as a solo artist. Then last year I got on a real downer because nothing was happening. I stopped going out of the house and just vegetated. That's when I saw the ad for Five in *The Stage*.

"When I joined Five I was still with my girlfriend and she was worried that the band would change things between us. I was sincere when I said

"I DON'T KNOW WHY, BUT I'VE ALWAYS HAD AN EYE FOR OLDER WOMEN. EVEN WHEN I WAS YOUNGER I'D BE OGLING THE LIKES OF RAQUEL WELCH WHILE MY MATES THOUGHT KYLIE WAS THE BUSINESS."

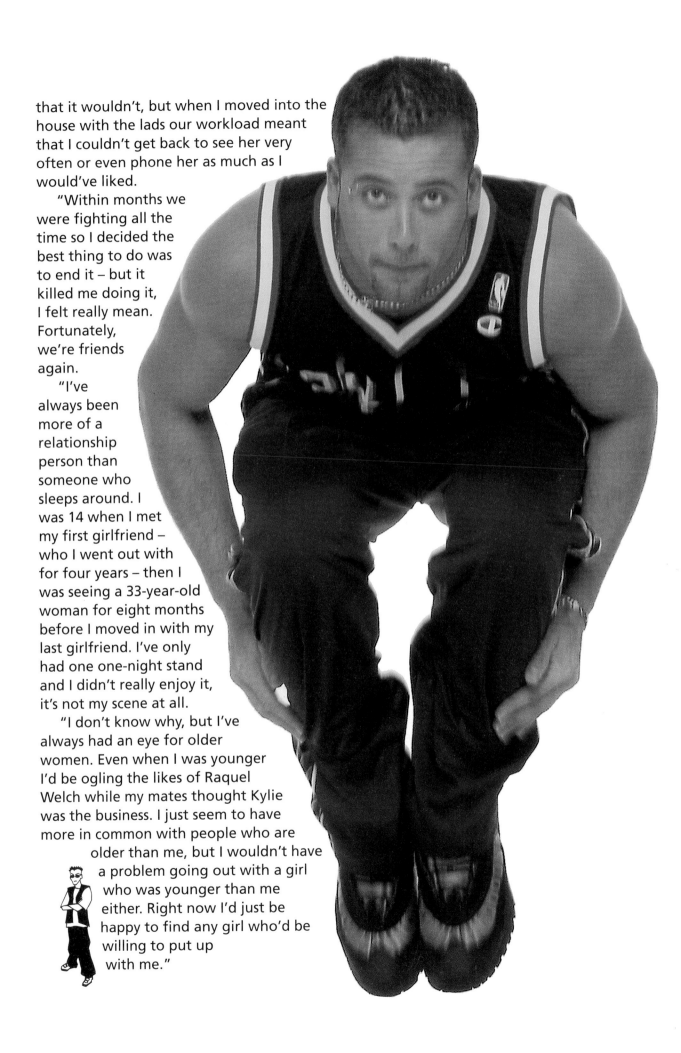

that it wouldn't, but when I moved into the house with the lads our workload meant that I couldn't get back to see her very often or even phone her as much as I would've liked.

"Within months we were fighting all the time so I decided the best thing to do was to end it – but it killed me doing it, I felt really mean. Fortunately, we're friends again.

"I've always been more of a relationship person than someone who sleeps around. I was 14 when I met my first girlfriend – who I went out with for four years – then I was seeing a 33-year-old woman for eight months before I moved in with my last girlfriend. I've only had one one-night stand and I didn't really enjoy it, it's not my scene at all.

"I don't know why, but I've always had an eye for older women. Even when I was younger I'd be ogling the likes of Raquel Welch while my mates thought Kylie was the business. I just seem to have more in common with people who are older than me, but I wouldn't have a problem going out with a girl who was younger than me either. Right now I'd just be happy to find any girl who'd be willing to put up with me."

FACTFILE

JASON

1. **Sex** Top of my agenda.

2. **Drinking** My favourite pastime.

3. **Politics** I check up on them every now and then.

4. **Music** Music is my life.

5. **Fashion** I never have and never will follow fashion. I wear what I want and what I feel comfortable in.

6. **Money** I love money, but I could live without it.

7. **Fame** Has its ups and downs.

8. **Sport** Often watched, hardly ever played.

9. **Women** Superb.

10. **Love** Sometimes cruel, sometimes kind.

11. **Best buy** My sampler for my recording studio.

12. **Favourite accessory** My jewellery - i.e. watch, eye ring, etc.

13. **Favourite hang-out** A club called 'East' in Sweden.

14. **Favourite romantic moment** That would be telling.

15. **Worst buy** Set of lockpicks costing £120.

16. **Love girls who** Have a sense of humour.

17. **Hate girls who** Use vulgar language.

18. **Favourite take-away...** Indian and Chinese.

19. **Favourite record of all time...** Too many to mention.

20. **Worst record of all time** 'Nothing's Gonna Change My Love For You' – Glenn Medeiros.

21. **Worst habit** Losing my temper.

22. **Favourite part of the female body** Everything.

23. **Monthly mobile phone bill** £40

Favourite romantic moment... THAT WOULD BE TELLING.

Worst buy... SET OF LOCKILES. COSTING £120.

Love girls who... HAVE A SENSE OF HUMOUR.

Hate girls who... USE VULGAR LANGUAGE.

Favourite take-away... INDIAN + CHINESE

Favourite record of all time... TOO MANY TO MENTION.

Worst Record of all time... "NOTHING'S GONNA CHANGE MY LOVE" GLEN MADEIRO.

Worst habit... LOSING MY TEMPER

Favourite part of the female body... EVERYTHING.

Monthly mobile phone bill... £40.

Worst job ever had... WORKING IN A WAREHOUSE.

One thing I'd change about myself... SCARE ON MY RIGHT JAWLINE

24 **Worst job ever had**
Working in a warehouse.

25 **One thing I'd change about myself**
Scar on my right jaw-line.

26 **Biggest regret**
Being horrible to everybody when I was thirteen.

27 **Proudest achievement**
Producing my first demo.

RICHARD NEVILLE

Good looking, charming and friendly – only he doesn't see it himself!

RICHARD NEVILLE defies the traditional route that handsome, talented men usually take in that he truly isn't full of himself. He may rate as one of the most popular members of Five, but Rich spends his spare time jumping from one confidence crisis to another.

Born in Solihull, Birmingham, his parents, Kim and Peter, split when he was two but his mother later re-married Rich's stepfather, Derek. Rich, together with his elder brother, Dave, and sister, Tracey, spent much of their youth in a pub – but only because their mum was the landlady.

Friendly, enthusiastic and always optimistic, Rich is one of the easiest members of Five to talk to, so make sure you are sitting comfortably...

"I grew up in a pub called the Crab Mill that my mum and stepdad still run in Bromsgrove and I had the best childhood. From the age of three I've been hanging out with my brother and his mates, who are eight years older than me, and as a result I'd say I'm pretty mature for my years.

5 YEARS OLD AND DEEP IN THOUGHT

"My brother taught me about all the things I should never have known about at an early age.

"I was a bit of a lad in my teens. I liked going out, meeting girls and bunking the odd lesson or two, but nothing that really got me into trouble. I went to a public school called Bromsgrove School, which is quite posh.

"Mum and Dad worked hard and missed out on having a smart car and things so they could send me there. We worked really long hours at school, Monday to Friday from 8.30 a.m. to 6 p.m. and Saturday from 8.30 a.m. to 4 p.m. I found the work quite hard and I had awful handwriting. My reports always said 'Richard could do better. He talks too much and is disruptive'. Later I discovered I had dyslexia, which accounts for my love of music and acting over academic work.

"I joined the National Theatre when I was 14 and was in a play called *Body Work*, which we took to the Edinburgh Festival. I liked the acting but I jacked it in because it was such a mission to come down to London every week for rehearsals.

"If I'm honest, music has always been my first love. I remember the first single I bought was 'Rent' by the Pet Shop Boys. I got it home, put it on the stereo and this song called 'I Want A Dog' came on. I went mad and walked 25 minutes back into town to take it back. They were really sweet in the shop and explained my mistake – I'd been playing the B side!

"I was in a band at school called Anal Beard (yeah, I know – bad name) and we played local gigs. We weren't very good but it was my first experience of music. My ambition now is to write songs. I have plenty of ideas for songs in my head and as soon as I get some money I'm going to buy a guitar to help me get them down on paper.

"I've always had a girlfriend – until I joined Five, that is. It's completely killed my love life because we're never in one place long enough to meet anyone and really get to know them.

"I've only had one real love. I was 16 and it's something I'll never forget. We were together for a year, but we then started arguing and eventually split up. I've been looking for the same sort of feeling I had with her ever since. I go out with girls, but I haven't found anything that compares with it...not yet, anyway."

"IF I'M HONEST, MUSIC HAS ALWAYS BEEN MY FIRST LOVE. I REMEMBER THE FIRST SINGLE I BOUGHT WAS 'RENT' BY THE PET SHOP BOYS."

FACTFILE RICHARD

1. **Sex** Yes please! I love it!

2. **Drinking** I do it, but everything in moderation (ha, ha).

3. **Politics** A necessary evil.

4. **Music** Life wouldn't be the same without it, in fact, life wouldn't be life without it.

5. **Fashion** I'm not a victim, but I like nice clothes.

6. **Money** The way the world is, you need it and it's nice to have, but I would rather be happy and poor than rich and unhappy.

7. **Fame** Something I have always wanted.

8. **Sport** Any chance to get my kit off!

9. **Women** I'll never be able to work them out, but I love them!

10. **Love** Deep and it hurts, intense but worth it. If it's going to happen, you can't stop it.

11. **Biggest extravagance** A night in a five-star hotel, Valentine's Day 1996.

12. **Best buy** 'Tabs' sweets, 3p a pack – BARGAIN!

13. **Favourite accessory** My jewellery, all bought by family, so of very sentimental value.

14. **Favourite hang-out** My brother's flat, because I don't have to wash up there.

15. **Favourite romantic moment** Yesterday and Valentine's Day 1996.

16. **Worst buy** Chips at our local chippy – they're nasty.

17. **Love girls who** Are girls.

18. **Hate girls who** Are dizzy, indecisive and turn me down (ha, ha). To be honest I can't say I hate anyone and I never have.

19. **Favourite take-away** Chinese.

20. **Favourite record of all time** Pearl Jam – 'Jeremy'.

㉑ **Worst record of all time** Mr Blobby.

㉒ **Worst habit** Biting my nails.

㉓ **Favourite part of the female body** I love it all.

㉔ **Monthly mobile phone bill** Too obscene to print.

㉕ **Worst job ever had** Never had a job I didn't enjoy.

㉖ **One thing I'd change about myself** I'm too impatient.

㉗ **Biggest regret** A night in Sweden, walking home with some tramps – I'll say no more.

㉘ **Proudest achievement** FIVE!

SCOTT ROBINSON

8 YEARS OLD, AT DISNEYLAND WITH NICOLA (LEFT), HAYLEY (RIGHT)

Low confidence? Quiet? Timid? – So you haven't met Scott then!

SCOTT ROBINSON was born to be a pop star – and he's been in training for it all his life. Born on 22 November 1979 in Basildon, Essex, where he lived until he was 17 with his parents, Mick and Sue, and his two elder sisters, Nicola and Hayley, Scott is the band's spokesman – mainly due to his ability to talk the hind legs off a donkey.

Some say his stage school training and early stints at acting have made him the fast talking and highly sociable sort of bloke he is today, but he insists he's always been this 'full-on and annoying'.

'Shy' is most definitely not a word you'd associate with Scott, as he'll tell you himself...

"I was eight when I first went on stage at an audition with my sister, Nicola, at the Towngate Theatre in Basildon, Essex for a production called *Monty Moonbeam's Magnificent Mission*. It was almost a disaster, I clammed up and burst into tears – which was not the most promising of starts to what I hope will be a dazzling career!

"My mum and dad say I was showing off from the moment I could walk. They used to dress me up as Boy George and Mr T and I'd lay on shows for anyone who'd watch – especially if we were on holiday and there was a talent night on.

MY SCHOOL PHOTO AT 10 YEARS!

"Nicola was into performing more than I was when we were kids and she did lots of local shows and the National Youth Music Theatre.

"I followed in her shoes and joined the theatre when I was 14 to do a show called *Whistle In The Wind*, which toured Edinburgh and London. It was brilliant, but disaster struck when my voice broke towards the end of the run – so I decided to leave.

"But the tour made me realize I couldn't go back to an ordinary comprehensive school and so I started at The Sylvia Young Stage School. I'd always hated school because I had a real problem with spelling. It wasn't until I went to Sylvia's that I discovered I was dyslexic, which explained why my academic work had always been so bad.

"It was a relief to know there was a reason for it and that I wasn't just thick, but I still struggled with my exams. The only thing I wrote on my maths GCSE paper was 'I am a fish', because, like me, a fish only has a ten second memory!

"Exams aside, I loved Sylvia's. I made some really good mates there and I was doing some TV ads and roles in programmes like *Casualty* and *EastEnders* (I played a racist thug who terrified Gita while Sanjay was away). My first TV appearance was actually with Hale and Pace and I did *Peter Pan* in the West End before I joined Five.

"One of my mates at stage school was Simon Bright who plays Baz on *Live & Kicking*. I think a lot of my class will do well, especially when you consider who was studying a few years above me. There was Dani Behr, Emma Bunton from the Spice Girls, Mel, Natalie and Nicole from All Saints, Denise Van Outen and Samantha Janus. Not bad, eh?

"It was while I was at Sylvia's that I really got into chart music (I've never made any pretence about being into 'cool' music – as the lads will tell you). I really loved Wet Wet Wet, especially Marti Pellow.

"I used to impersonate him and I even got down to the last audition for *Stars In Their Eyes*. I'm glad I didn't

"MY MUM AND DAD SAY I WAS SHOWING OFF FROM THE MOMENT I COULD WALK. THEY USED TO DRESS ME UP AS BOY GEORGE AND MR T AND I'D LAY ON SHOWS FOR ANYONE WHO'D WATCH." 5 SCOTT get picked now – can you imagine the grief I'd get from the lads?

"It's not as if they don't give me enough stick – especially about my confidence with girls. They reckon I can go up to any girl and start talking, but that's not entirely true. I'm quite shy around a girl I really like.

"I've only had one serious relationship and when it ended I was devastated. It was just after I'd joined Five and I'd been seeing this girl for six months. She said she'd stick by me when I got into the group...but basically she didn't.

"A few weeks after I'd moved in with the lads we were recording in Sweden when she finished with me over the phone. She said she didn't think she could handle the stress of going out with someone who was away from home a lot and in a band that was gaining as much attention as Five. I was distraught.

"There's one track we recorded which I'm not even on because I couldn't talk or sing, I was that upset. I looked a mess too, the blood vessels in my eyes had burst because I'd been crying so much.

"Oh God, I'm in danger of getting soppy now, time to go..."

FACTFILE

SCOTT

① **Sex** Yes, if you have blue eyes.

② **Drinking** Stella – lots of it.

③ **Politics** I'm a Labour man myself.

④ **Music** Don't get me started, I could talk all day.

⑤ **Fashion** I'm not a victim. I wear whatever's on the floor.

⑥ **Money** Hope to have lots of it very, very soon, so keep buying the records!

⑦ **Fame** 'I Wanna Live Forever'

⑧ **Sport** Basketball because football's awful.

⑨ **Women** Form an orderly queue please, no fighting ladies!

⑩ **Favourite accessory** I feel naked without my jewellery.

⑪ **Favourite hang-out** The pub in Essex.

⑫ **Favourite romantic moment** Meal for two with my ex.

⑬ **Worst buy** Meal for two with my ex.

⑭ **Love girls who** Agree to go out with me.

⑮ **Hate girls who** Argue about anything and everything and I don't like girls who are a pushover.

⑯ **Favourite take-away** Pizza – just a margherita.

⑰ **Favourite record of all time** Any 80s love song.

⑱ **Worst record of all time** 'Doop' – Doop

⑲ **Worst habit** Sleeping on the way to work.

20 **Favourite part of the female body** Eyes and lips.

21 **Monthly mobile phone bill** £135!!!

22 **Worst job ever had** Working in a burger van but I do love burgers.

23 **One thing I'd change about myself** My hairy legs and feet.

24 **Biggest regret** Meal for two with my ex.

25 **Proudest achievement** Getting into Five.

ABS

BREEN

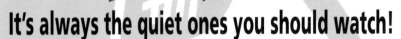

ME AT 1 YEAR OLD

It's always the quiet ones you should watch!

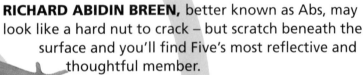

ME BEING MICHAEL JACKSON

RICHARD ABIDIN BREEN, better known as Abs, may look like a hard nut to crack – but scratch beneath the surface and you'll find Five's most reflective and thoughtful member.

A Londoner, born in Enfield on 29 June 1979, he was raised alone by his half-Irish mother, Kay and, as a child, saw little of his Turkish father, Turan.

Polite to a fault, with manners that would impress even the Queen, Abs is wise beyond his years – but beneath his mild exterior lies a determined and very focused individual.

As he'll tell you, there's more to Abs than meets the eye...

"It's always been just me and my mum. I was raised as an only child in a single-parent family. My childhood wasn't what you'd call conventional. My mum and dad were never married and Dad's always been in and out of my life. I've only really got to know him over the last two years and we get on well, but obviously I am much closer to my mum.

"Mum says she knew I'd end up performing because I was singing and dancing as soon as I was physically able – I used to have glittery socks and white gloves and I'd impersonate Michael Jackson day and night. I never used to walk around the flat we lived in – I'd moonwalk!

"I got really into tap dancing when I was a kid after I went along to watch Mum doing a class. She asked me to join in and I was reluctant at first because I thought it was a girl's hobby, but once I got into it I loved it.

"Needless to say though, tap class wasn't something I asked other kids on our estate to come along to. Where we lived was rough. Often in the middle of the night there were police sirens going off and people swearing and screaming, but somehow I always managed not to get involved in any trouble.

"School was fine for me, I never loved it but I certainly didn't hate it and I got reasonable exam results. I very rarely bunked off and if I did it was only to go out with my cousin who had a car, which I thought was really impressive. We'd spend all day driving around listening to jungle music thinking we were really cool. Sad, I know.

"I'm quite close to my cousins, even on my dad's side, but I must admit I find it a bit uncomfortable visiting my Turkish relatives because I have to get into 'Turkish mode'. I find it difficult because I don't know as much as I should about the history and culture. I can hold a conversation in Turkish – but apart from that I'm pretty ignorant.

"When I left school I knew I wanted to either sing, dance or act, so I auditioned for a scholarship at the Italia Conti Stage School, where people like Louise, Naomi Campbell and Martine McCutcheon studied – but they turned me down. Determined not to be defeated I started attending their Saturday school and auditioned again a year later, when I was finally accepted. I was so happy. I felt that, at last, I'd found my niche in life.

"I met some great people at Conti's – including my girlfriend, Danielle – but I was only there for three months before I joined Five. I'm still with Danielle and I know she likes me for me, not just because I'm in a band. She's my first serious girlfriend and she makes me smile – but I don't get to see her as much as I used to.

"I don't know if what we have will last forever because we're still both so young, but I don't think I'd know how to go about being single again. The thought of chatting up a girl fills me with horror. I've never chatted anyone up in my life and when I see other blokes doing it I cringe. I know Rich is rubbish at pulling, but even he would look good next to me!"

"I'M QUITE CLOSE TO MY COUSINS, EVEN ON MY DAD'S SIDE, BUT MUST ADMIT I FIND IT A BIT UNCOMFOFORTABLE VISITING MY TURKISH RELATIVES BECAUSE I HAVE TO GET INTO 'TURKISH' MODE."

FACTFILE

ABS

① **Sex** Is better if you love the person you're doing it with!!

② **Drinking** I only drink non-alcoholic drinks, but I love watching the others get drunk.

③ **Politics** I don't really understand the games that go on, but I liked John Major's hairstyle!

④ **Music** I'm into anything with a big bass.

⑤ **Fashion** My favourite type of clothing is casual everyday stuff.

⑥ **Money** Gimmee, Gimmee, Gimmee!

⑦ **Fame** I'm still trying to get used to it but don't think I ever will.

⑧ **Sport** I like playing it on my Playstation!

⑨ **Women** They're great but they cost you loads.

⑩ **Love** Thinking of the person every minute of the day and wanting to be with them.

⑪ **Homelife** I'm a Cancerian so I love being at home with friends and family and try to get back whenever I can.

⑫ **On Five** What a bunch of lunatics.

⑬ **Hates** Smoking while eating.

⑭ **Biggest extravagance** Running outside in the street with only my boxer shorts on in the rain, trying out my new radio control car that I got for Christmas.

⑮ **Best buy** A pocket game for 50p down the market.

⑯ **Favourite accessory** My bracelet! It was given to me for getting into Five.

⑰ **Favourite hang-out** Bed.

⑱ **Favourite romantic moment** Walking down a street in Paris on Christmas Day in the rain with my girl.

⑲ **Worst buy** A pair of £250 contact lenses that blew away in the wind.

⑳ **Love girls who** Are feminine.

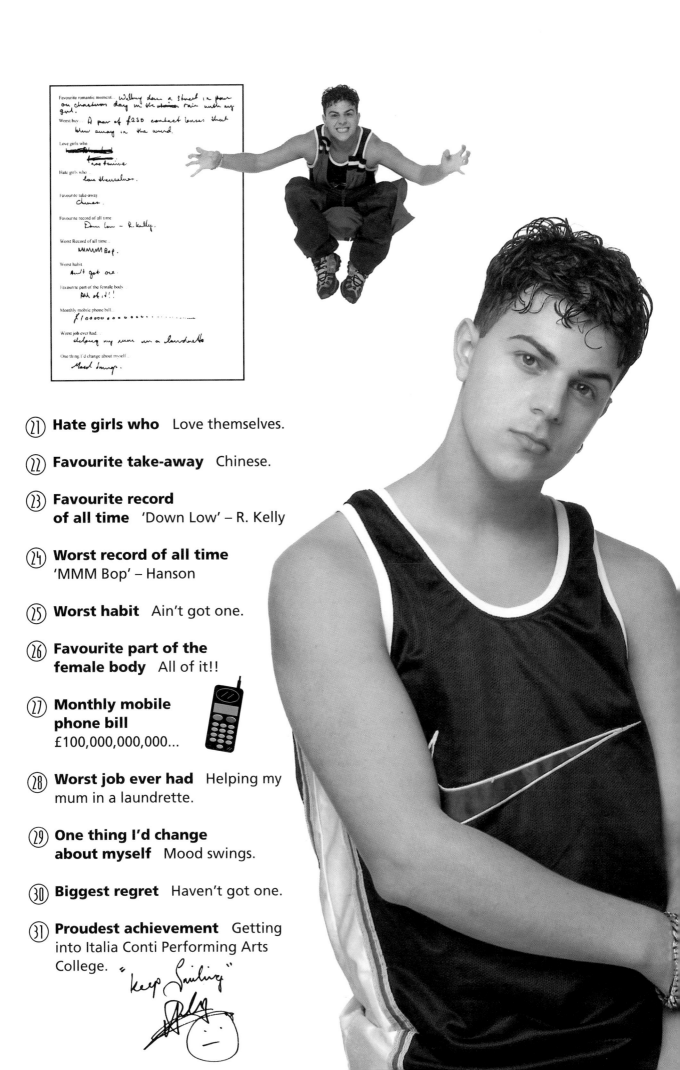

㉑ **Hate girls who**   Love themselves.

㉒ **Favourite take-away**   Chinese.

㉓ **Favourite record of all time**   'Down Low' – R. Kelly

㉔ **Worst record of all time**   'MMM Bop' – Hanson

㉕ **Worst habit**   Ain't got one.

㉖ **Favourite part of the female body**   All of it!!

㉗ **Monthly mobile phone bill**   £100,000,000,000...

㉘ **Worst job ever had**   Helping my mum in a laundrette.

㉙ **One thing I'd change about myself**   Mood swings.

㉚ **Biggest regret**   Haven't got one.

㉛ **Proudest achievement**   Getting into Italia Conti Performing Arts College.   "Keep Smiling"

FIVE ON THE FIVE

They live together, they work together, they've even cried together (but more of that later). Scott, Sean, Abs, J and Rich probably know each other better than they know themselves – but what do they really think of each other?

Here they spill the beans on that and so much more...

Who has the worst or most annoying habits?
J and **SEAN**: Scott.
SCOTT: Yeah, it probably is me because I make loads of stupid noises – I annoy myself at times!
RICH: It drives me mad when I get home from work and I just want to watch the TV and he's whooping and yelping like a nutter.
SCOTT: I know it drives you all mad, but I treat it as my hobby!

"SEAN HAS GOT TO BE THE LAZIEST PERSON ANY OF US HAVE EVER MET."

J: Abs has started turning up late for things recently and he keeps pinching our nipples. That gets on my nerves.
RICH: It's not hard to get on J's nerves – he's so moody, his moods affect the whole band and he gets almost suicidal.
ABS: And Sean has got to be the laziest person any of us have ever met.
J: He knocked a drink over the carpet the other day and anyone else would have mopped it up – not Sean – he just threw an empty cig packet over it. He is the laziest person on the face of this earth.
SCOTT: Rich is the worst for getting up in the morning...
J: I get everyone up in the morning and I make sure I wake Rich first because I know he's guaranteed to fall

back to sleep while we're getting ready and make us all at least twenty minutes late. He makes weird noises first thing in the morning as well, he sounds like a tortured animal.

ABS: I've got to say J, you scare me when you wake me up. Your voice is so deep first thing it's like being woken up by Barry White!

Who's the most explosive member of the band?

ALL: J.

RICH: You start to worry when he takes his eye-ring out because you know he's getting ready for a fight. He hasn't hit any of us yet, but it's come close.

J: Rich is the peacemaker. He butts in on rows and says, 'Guys, guys...let's be mates.'."

RICH: They say I'm like Neil from *The Young Ones*.

Who's the most romantic member of the band?

RICH: It's probably me, then Abs, then Scott, and J and Sean would be joint last.

J: Rich talks about girls romantically, but I probably talk about sex more than the others. Sean's the most sensitive. When we were working in Denmark, doing two tracks with the producers Cult Father and Joe, Sean went on his own to a club – every night! He met a bar girl there who was in her mid-twenties and she told him her whole life story. He felt so sorry for her that he decided he was going to take her away from her difficult life style – and

"THEY SAY I'M LIKE NEIL FROM THE YOUNG ONES."

every night he'd come back to the hotel and spend hours talking about how he was going to take her back to England.

Who shares hotel rooms while you're on the road?

ABS: It used to be J and Sean, Rich and Scott and I'd have a room to myself. But now Rich has his own room and I share with Scott because we both like to go to bed earlier than the others.

SEAN: I share with J because we like raiding the mini-bar and staying up all night.

J: What about that time we were having a drink and all ended up crying. We were drinking this weird stuff and because we were feeling so many different emotions it made us all burst into tears. I

really feel that this was the night the band bonded.

Who is the most competitive?

ABS: J always wants to win. We went go-karting together and everyone was racing for the fastest lap time. We were all having a laugh, but J took it really seriously. Too seriously!

J: You're only saying that because I'm the only one with a driving licence – and I beat you all. To be honest, we're as competitive as each other – we all broke the rules when we were go-karting because everyone desperately wanted to win. Sean tries to pretend he's laid-back, but even he can't resist fighting to come first.

Has anyone ever threatened to leave the group?

J: Me and Sean have – loads of times. I've actually packed my bags four times. Once, when we were living at the first house, I stormed out and drove to my dad's place – but he wasn't in, so I had to come back.

ABS: My mum phoned J and Sean to try and talk them round. It was really sweet.

THE BEST BITS

SO FAR...

About to unfold are the golden memories that Rich, J, Sean, Abs and Scott will recite to their grandchildren. These are the best bits of their journey so far – the highs, the lows and the nights that were a bit hazy in places...

GETTING THE GIG...

J: The best moment had to be when we were told we were in the band.

RICH: I remember just looking at J and I'll never forget the expression on our faces. We were being filmed at the time and I was crouching down and you see me stand up into shot with the cheekiest smile on my face.

GETTING ON...

J: We recorded 'Slam' in Sweden with these brilliant producers called Deniz Pop and Herbie Crichlow and it

was during that trip that I think we really bonded.

RICH: Definitely. We'd been in the studio all day, which in itself was a treat because we'd all dreamed about working in a proper studio. When we went back to the hotel that night it was like all the pieces of a jigsaw puzzle fell into place.

SCOTT: There was this funny little nightclub in the basement of our hotel – it was really naff – but we went along and by the end of the night we were dancing to all these mad tunes and diving on each other and mucking

"WE RECORDED 'SLAM' IN SWEDEN WITH THESE BRILLIANT PRODUCERS" 5 JASON

about. We didn't stop smiling and laughing.

SEAN: I think I even got up for a bit of a groove...

SCOTT: We all went to bed with smiles on our faces. That was probably the best night out we've ever had.

GETTING ON STAGE...

RICH: Our first performance – at the Radio One Roadshow in Cheltenham – is something I'll never forget. We turned up expecting no-one to give us a second look – but we were blown away by the reaction.

SCOTT: As soon as we got out of the van all these girls started screaming and asking for our autographs. I was amazed that they even knew who we were.

ABS: One girl even asked for my bottle of water – and told me my backwash tasted lovely!

J: It was the first time any of us had signed an autograph and every time we went near the crowd a cheer went up. We kept doing it all afternoon, running up one at a time – it was such a buzz.

RICH: We made Radio One history that day because we'd only been invited on as the warm up act and the crowd liked us so much that the DJ, Dave Pearce, stepped in and got us on air later that afternoon.

SEAN: We had to drive to Cornwall afterwards and all the way there we just kept saying 'That was amazing!'

GETTING AWAY...

ABS: When we were recording in Stockholm we used to walk past a big lake on our way back from the studio. It was freezing cold and out of the blue J took off all his clothes and jumped into the water. The next thing we knew, Sean had taken all his clothes off and jumped in too. What nutters!

J: The water was freezing. Me and Sean started to go blue so we had to climb out quick before we froze to death. The other lads carried our clothes and we had to walk back to the hotel in our boxer shorts.

ABS: It was so embarrassing back at the hotel. Sean and J were dripping wet, in their pants, and all the guests stared at us as we ran past them to the lift.

GETTING IN FRONT OF THE VIDEO CAMERA...

J: Most of the first video we shot for 'Slam' was unusable. It was very dark and considered too hip-hop, but a few frames made it into the final edit.

SEAN: One of the scenes

"IT WAS FREEZING COLD AND OUT OF THE BLUE J TOOK OFF ALL HIS CLOTHES AND JUMPED INTO THE WATER. THE NEXT THING WE KNEW, SEAN HAD TAKEN ALL HIS CLOTHES OFF AND JUMPED IN TOO." 5 ABS

was set on the back of a truck and we had to drive around London in it with 'Slam' blaring out of the speakers. I've never seen so many people do a double-take in my life. It was brilliant!

GETTING THE RIGHT TEAM IN PLACE...

J: I know it sounds corny, but we really do have the best people working with us. They go above and beyond the call of duty making sure that everything is the best it can be. For me, Herbie Crichlow is one of the best people I've met. He's one of our writer/producers and I clicked with him immediately.

SCOTT: The people at the record company are cool too. Our head of marketing, David Joseph, is a nice geezer and he has our respect.

SEAN: Dave Shack, the head of Radio and TV Promotions, is the one we go to the pub with most. He's a blinding fella, a genuine guy who sees us as people and not just another band.

RICH: On top of that we've got a great press officer in Emma Nicholson and a brilliant TV plugger called Sacha Relfe – and of course we really take our hats off to Simon Cowell, he's got a real vision for Five.

J: But Chris and Bob deserve the most respect because we're not the easiest group to manage at times – and we wouldn't be here without them.

YOU AIN'T SEEN NOTHIN' YET!

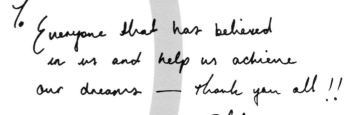

To. Everyone that has believed
in us and help us achieve
our dreams — thank you all !!

Hi

Still awake? goooood.
Thanx for buying the 5ivE book
I hope you enjoyed it - WE DID
Im going To Tell What's next for Five
So...oooh Someone's taking the pen away

lots of love

In the short time that Five have been together they've achieved three hit singles, picked up one of the most coveted awards in the music industry and released their debut album to critical acclaim.

The world is theirs for the taking – and take it they will!

Their ambition, like their music, knows no bounds. Individually, every member is blessed with enough talent to ensure they could easily have made it as stars in their own right – collectively, they are unstoppable.

As we close the final chapter of this book Sean, Rich, Abs, J and Scott are merely closing the first chapter in what will be an extraordinary journey for them all.

What you have heard, read and seen of them so far serves only as an appetizer for what is yet to come...

This past year has been an incredible experience for the Lads and I, and it could not have been possible without YOU, the fans. Thanks sooo much and stick with us, the best is yet to come!

Loads of Love

Rich

A GREAT BIG THANX TO EVERYBODY FOR SUPPORTING US, BUYING THE SINGLES & FOR JUST BEING THERE.

ALL MY LOVE

J

Thank you very much for your Support. Thankyou for buying our Single if you did. Hopefully we will have your Support forever.

love

Sean

ACKNOWLEDGEMENTS

ABS
Thank you to: all my family – Mum, Dad, cousins, aunts and uncles for believing in me; Courtnie and Tina for the bite marks; all my boys – Errol, Ilker, Toy and the rest of you for helping to keep me down-to-earth; Danielle for putting up with me; Bob and Chris for making it happen; Paul Domaine for the moves; everyone at Safe Management; RCA Records and to Five – let's do this!

RICH
Thanks to: Mum, Dad, Dave, Tracey, Derek, Robert, Nan, aunts and uncles and all my mates for believing in me and making sacrifices to help me get where I am; everyone at RCA for their help; all the producers and people we've worked with; Paul Domaine; a big one to Bob and Chris and Safe Management and to the band – it's been great and I'll never forget it!

SEAN
Thank you to: all my family; everyone at RCA (you know who you are); Paul Domaine, and of course to Bob and Chris (and Safe Management) for all the hard work, and to the band – take it easy!

SCOTT
Thanks to: Mum and Dad for supporting me in everything I've done – and for putting up with such a nutcase; my sisters Nicola and Hayley for not moaning about the money it cost to send me to acting school – one day I'll pay you back; the rest of my family and friends; Bob and Chris for giving me the chance – I couldn't have done it without you; Simon Cowell and everyone at RCA; all the people behind Five – Safe Management, Paul Domaine, the fans, the parents and the press and to the other lads – thanks for being as much of a fruitcake as I am!

J
A massive thank you to: Mum, Dad and all my family; all my friends; everyone at RCA who has put so much into Five; Paul Domaine; Bob and Chris for doing it all; Safe Management, and to the other lads – Yes!

AUTHORS

JANE PRESTON is a former dancer, actress, radio presenter and newspaper journalist who currently works as a mother, author and freelance writer.

KATE THORNTON is a former *Smash Hits* editor and *Daily Mirror* columnist who currently works as a television presenter and freelance writer.